THE
PEOPLE
SECRET

Published by Mindstir Media, LLC

1931 Woodbury Ave. #182 | Portsmouth, New Hampshire 03801 | USA

1.800.767.0531 | www.mindstirmedia.com

Printed in the United States of America

ISBN-13: 978-0-9975435-6-8

Library of Congress Control Number: 2016906655

MINDSTIR MEDIA

THE
PEOPLE
SECRET

THE 2 BY 4 APPROACH
TO BUILDING A BUSINESS

JIM LIGGETT & JACK HOBAN

CONTENTS

PREFACE

This story began 20 years ago when Jack Hoban, a UPS communications manager, and Jim Liggett, a UPS employee relations manager, discussed the challenge of people relations. They had worked on several employee relations projects and had a unique view about how to make work more fun and more productive. One project in particular was a training session which was planned in advance of the annual employee opinion survey.

The training started as Jim entered a conference room dressed in a full safari outfit, complete with pith helmet and jungle sounds. He carried a box marked "top secret" with a parrot on top, its beak wrapped in duct tape. "He was starting to talk," admitted Jim.

Jim told the audience of about 60 that the box contained the "secret" to employee relations and a winning score. He also told the managers he would reveal the "secret" at the end of the day. He then took the group through an employee relations training session.

Later that day, Jim pulled a number of items out of the box. Most needed little explanation. They were obvious tools every manager has at their disposal. This was when "The People Secret" was born.

And what were the results of that training? The district scored one of the highest indexes in the country and one of the most improved. The results were not the direct result of the presentation, but it had reminded the managers of the importance of building strong relationships with their people through daily interactions. The managers took what they already knew and put the "secret" into action. One other result of improved people relations was improved performance.

Hopefully, this book is a useful tool for young managers who are finding their way through a new management assignment—or even seasoned managers who may need a refresher course in the area of people relations.

Every business has three areas of focus: a product or service, work processes and people. Most businesses do the first two right. Many struggle with the third. They focus on building their business, and ignore building their people. And as Zig Ziglar said, "You don't build a business—you build people—and then people build the business."

As you read this book, you will realize that "The People Secret" is not a secret at all. We all know the right way to lead—and that there is no such thing as employee relations - only human relations.

Jack Hoban and Jim Liggett retired from UPS with a combined 54 years of management experience. They understand that the best management people possessed strong people skills as well as strong operations skills. But it was their people skills that separated them from the rest.

Jim Liggett has over 30 years of management experience ranging from business operations to human resources. He holds a Master of Arts Degree in Organizational Management and was Professional Faculty in the Carey Business School at Johns Hopkins University for seven years. He was also Chairman of the Radio Reading Network of Maryland for 20 years. There is a phrase that "the process will produce what the process will produce." Jim believes this is true only if there are good people behind the process. Jim lives in Maryland with his wife, Judy. They have one daughter, Pam.

Jack Hoban worked in management at UPS for over 23 years, mostly in internal communications, public relations and employee retention. He has an English/Journalism degree from the University of Delaware and an MBA in Management from Eastern University. He is currently the safety director for Sposato Landscape, Inc. in Milton, Delaware, and also works as a freelance writer. He also knows all the words to Bob Dylan's `Subterranean Homesick Blues'. He and his wife, Denise, live in Lewes, Delaware. They have two children, Lauren and Alison.

LOOKING BACK, LOOKING FORWARD

Linda didn't know it, but she was about to be fired.

Her boss, John, the director of marketing at Perryman-Willis, had called her into his office. Sitting with him was Marianne, the human resources manager, and she had Linda's severance package ready to review. John was nervous and pained and had always reminded Linda of the Lion in the Wizard of Oz—but without the good looks and kind heart.

He had not been happy with her work results since she got promoted a little over a year ago. This was the latest and last in a series of talks he would have with Linda about her job performance. John had run out of patience.

In previous talks with Linda, she blamed her people for her poor results. "They don't give me a heads up to potential problems. Could I fire a few of them to get the others' attention and bring in better team players?" John's answer was always to continue working with them.

Linda came to the company three years earlier with an impressive background: a progressive work history, an education from a top university with a double major in marketing and management. She interned at Perryman-Willis during her senior year and landed an entry-level supervisor position. Two years later, she was promoted to product marketing manager.

But she was failing miserably in all areas of her operation: people, processes and performance. Feedback from her people indicated she was aloof and a poor communicator. They claimed she never told them what was going on and hoarded information. Her people were unmotivated and said that she demonstrated no semblance of leadership. Even worse, they did not like or trust her.

"Linda, we are going to have to let you go," said John. "We are going to pay you for the rest of the month and cover your health care." Then John started talking about her management style, communication skills and the importance of results.

But Linda wasn't listening at this point. It was all a blur. She didn't care. She just wanted to get out of that office. "Wrong place, wrong time, and I guess wrong person for the job," she thought. Looking back, she reflected on the countless sleepless nights she endured worrying about her situation. And how the harder she worked, the worse things got.

She hit the street feeling empty and very much fired. She felt embarrassed, humiliated, desolate and hurt. "Sometimes bad things happen to good people." What would she tell her friends and her family? Yes, it was just a job. But her sense of failure could not be denied.

Linda also felt angry at the situation. She had failed but she certainly wouldn't take all the blame. Much of this disaster rested on her boss and her team. One of her people told her later that things went downhill from the start, when she didn't get up in front of them and properly introduce herself. "You just came in and said, 'Let's get to work.' Did you realize how that made us feel?" Linda would think about that later. Right now she was drowning in depression.

Linda just wanted to go home to Snert, her Jack Russell. Her two-year-old dog was about the only thing in her life that made sense and felt good. They went to the park. She threw the Frisbee, and watched Snert catch it and bring it back. To Snert it was second nature. The job she just left was the most unnatural experience of her working life. She'd get a grip eventually—just not today.

Weeks passed and it was now mid-September. While she had some savings and fairly low rent on her apartment, something needed to happen soon. She would be broke financially as well as emotionally before long. Her longest previous vacation was the permanent one of a teenager, before she started working at the age of 16 at the Bayview Theatre. "What was that Dickens adaptation set years ago?

Her friend Daniel had played Sydney Carton quite well," she remembered. Linda laughed a little and said to herself, it was *A Tale of Two Cities*, except for her this time in her life was pretty much the worst of times.

Linda looked for work in the usual places: job sites, LinkedIn, social media, even the newspapers. She sent a few resumes out to job listings, had one call back, but no interviews. All the jobs looked good on paper, but she knew that when she found a new one, the old problems would resurface if something didn't change. What had she missed? Did she even want to manage people again?

One thought kept reoccurring—her management style. What did John mean by that? What was her management style and what was wrong with it? She was smart, educated and had a great work ethic. She showed dedication and loyalty to the people she worked for. And she was a people person—always well-liked in school and at previous jobs. The people at Perryman-Willis liked her—until she became their boss.

"Maybe I'm not management material," she mused. Up until now, Linda thought a management career was pretty basic. "Go to school, get a degree, land a job and begin moving up the corporate ladder." It would be relatively easy—if it wasn't for all of these people problems.

Linda was raised in Connecticut. She had an older brother who was a finance manager in Boston, and terrific parents. They were not rich by any means. Her late father had worked as a manager in an insurance call center and her mom part-time in the school system. They were hard-working and honest. During her junior year in college her father suddenly passed away. Linda felt lost without his guidance and ability to say just the right thing at the right time. She had a partial scholarship, and between her various jobs, and some financial help from her mom, had completed her education with a minimal amount of debt. She took the job at Perryman-Willis thinking management would be easy. Just tell people what to do and they did it. She now knew that nothing could be farther from the truth.

South Haven was a neat little city of 75,000, with all the conveniences a single person wanted—excellent shopping, good restaurants and a vibrant nightlife. There was certainly enough activity to keep things interesting. Linda's favorite grocery store had an organic section that, thankfully, she could still afford. As she walked down the middle aisle Linda saw a familiar face. It was an old friend of her late father. She remembered they seemed close enough to be brothers. As she approached, his face beamed. The last time Linda had seen Charley was at the funeral. He was one of her father's pallbearers. They hugged and minutes later they were catching up on family news. Charley, sensing her despair, suggested they pause for coffee. Soon she was pouring out her feelings of sadness and hopelessness to him.

Linda thought back to family gatherings and remembered Charley as a regular shot-and-a-beer type of guy. Someone everyone liked. He also appeared to be very successful, yet never boastful. He always seemed concerned for other people and was a good listener.

"Linda, do you have any plans for tomorrow?" asked Charley.

"My calendar is pretty free these days," Linda said with a note of understatement.

"Why don't you come down to my shop around 8:00 a.m? It's located at 624 Green Street. You may find it interesting."

On her way home, Linda didn't know what to think of the offer—she would just show up and see what good old Charley had in mind. "What do I have to lose?" she thought.

The next day Linda arrived at the shop. In the middle of the entranceway a neat little garden and a small sign identified the place as the Cobart Company. After she walked inside, Sarah, the receptionist welcomed her and introduced herself. From a group of offices on the right, Charley gave her an enthusiastic wave. He was dressed in grey slacks, a white dress shirt and a blue blazer. Charley was clean cut, well-groomed and in his early 50's. Linda thought he looked relaxed, comfortable—like he belonged exactly where he was standing. They walked through a short hallway to a medium-size office with a large window overlooking the production floor. The facility was about 200 feet long with banners on the ceiling. The largest banner caught her attention. It read:

"We Build People Here."

After some small talk Charley pointed at a machine spinning out long, square metal bars. There were four people working around a large piece of equipment. "Those are going to the new high school they're building in Woodbridge," said Charley. "That's an important order for us. It's due out today. Looks like we are right on schedule. Come on, let's take a little walk."

As they walked Charley chatted with the people on the floor. He pointed out a few things that needed to be addressed and asked a lot of questions. When someone talked he listened intently.

Cobart made building materials for the construction industry and Charley gave Linda a quick tour of the shop floor. Linda saw the operation and thought it was a type of cellular job setup. There were different pods scattered about the warehouse. Each had dissimilar machines grouped into work centers. She knew this type of layout had become popular in modern factories and was valued for its flexibility and automation. "I did learn a few things in college," she remarked to herself.

"How many people work here?" asked Linda.

"Forty-three at various levels of job responsibility," said Charley. "Overall, they do a very good job. Not all are superstars, but our goal is to have everyone work to their potential. I'm very proud of them."

Charley stopped to talk to an employee. "We got that wiring problem in special products figured out," said the man.

"Great, Jack. Hey, how is your son?"

"He's fine, Charley. The tests all came back negative and he's going to be okay."

"Excellent. If you need anything, let me know. Jack, I would like you to meet Linda." They shook hands and with a tip of the cap, Jack went back to work.

"Best foreman in the entire company," said Charley. "I don't know what I would do without him."

Linda, a little perplexed, noticed that there seemed to be something missing. No follow-up questions on that wiring situation, or work that needed to be done today—just personal conversation.

When they arrived back at Charley's office, he got right to the point.

"Linda, I have a position open, and I thought after our conversation you might be interested. It's a management-trainee job. I know it may be a bit below your education, experience, and salary level. In fact, the salary is probably about half of what you made at Perryman-Willis. But it may be a good opportunity for you after what just happened."

Charlie continued. "I've found in my career that management can be the best job in the world or the worst. It depends on the situation you find yourself in and how you react to it. But there is also a way to change it from worst to best. If you sign on with me, I can teach you how to get to the 'best' part."

The possibility excited Linda. She had lived the "worst" part of management. Maybe she could learn the "best" part from Charley.

"I know I'm supposed to say give me a day to think about it, but I'm all in," she said.

"Great," said Charley. "When it comes to managing people, I believe this is the place where you can learn the secret, which I call the 2 by 4 approach to building a business."

"The 2 by 4 approach?" asked Linda. "What's that?"

"In good time," answered Charley. "That's something I want to show you—not just tell you. I will teach you how to develop your people and deliver world-class results. I'll teach you lessons you didn't learn in college—lessons that you knew all along but didn't trust yourself enough to use them at work."

"I can't wait," said Linda.

"Also, this assignment will only last for six months. HR will contact you later today. They'll direct you to the online site for the application process and take care of all the required legal documents. We'll start next Monday morning at 7:00."

On the ride home Linda experienced the euphoria that comes when someone actually wants you. She never felt that way with her old company. It was also quite a change from a marketing department to a manufacturing environment. A little daunting, but there was something about Charley that made her feel for the first time that someone had her best interests in mind. And what had Charley meant about her knowing the secret already but not trusting herself to use it at work? She couldn't wait for Monday to find out. She was about to learn the secret to managing people, or as he called it, the 2 by 4 approach.

BUILDING BLOCK 1: COMMUNICATION

Communication Builds Rapport

"People are the solution...not the problem." Charley

The following Monday morning at 6:30, Linda started off for the fifteen minute drive to 624 Green Street. Thoughts about her old job flashed through her head. Just a few months ago, eight people in a marketing department had reported to her and she had a level of responsibility that surprised her.

At first it all seemed manageable. But then strange things began to happen. When you start a new job everything seems easy, then you soon realize the more you learn about your position, the harder the job becomes. Linda found that the more she learned about the job, the more problems arose. What was easy at first became overwhelming. Then there was the people honeymoon, when everyone wanted to please you, which for her lasted about three months. At that point she knew her people skills were not strong enough to motivate her team let alone get them to take responsibility for their work.

There was also the matter of respect. She discovered that you cannot get it from your position alone. Quite the opposite. Linda grew angry when she thought about the people who had reported to her. She felt sabotaged by their continuous efforts to undermine her authority and demonstrate malicious obedience—where they would work as instructed and only do what they were told—not taking any initiative. Lastly, upper management became increasingly disillusioned with her. The harder she worked, the more she struggled, the more her goals drifted away. This time had to be different.

Cobart was a subsidiary of a larger firm based in Chicago. The facility was divided into shipping/receiving and production. There were three people in shipping and receiving, with 40 people involved in the production of building materials. In seven different pods, they were divided into various departments which included prefabrication, special products and standard units. What they produced varied from metal siding and frames to custom molding and components used in commercial buildings. They were profitable and thriving in an area where there was plenty of work but also plenty of competition.

Linda saw an immediate difference between her old work group's attitude and the people here at Cobart. Charley seemed like he had the easiest job in the world. She also noticed that problems appeared to amuse Charley. He looked at them as opportunities to get people to use their minds and come up with better solutions. It was not until the middle of the first week that she knew his actual job title, which was Plant Manager for The Cobart Company.

Management by Walking Around

"St. Jerome was fond of saying. To solve a problem, walk around."
                                                            Gregory McNamee

"I want you to spend time on the floor," said Charley. "Talk to people, learn what they do and ask questions. Just a little MBWA or management by walking around. Let me look at your shoes. You probably need better work shoes. A sturdy leather with good soles. You're going to do a lot of walking here. It's a big part of your job.

"Another piece of advice: keep work out of it as much as possible.

Observe their work, but these people know their jobs, so just get to know them on a personal level. Just go look." So off she went.

Charley looked surprised to find Linda sitting in her office about an hour later. "That was quick," he said. "What are you finding out?"

Linda was excited to bring him up to date. "I think I made some inroads. I talked to several people on the floor. Chan in special products and Judy and Walt in standard units."

"And?" asked Charlie.

"I told them all about my background, education and work experience. I think it went well."

"I see," said Charlie. "Let me ask you, what can you tell me about Judy?"

"Well, she looks like she knows what she's doing on the machine she operates. She seems to like her job."

"Does she have a family? What's her favorite sports team?" asked Charley.

"I don't know," answered Linda.

"How long has she worked here?"

"I don't know that either," said Linda, feeling more embarrassed.

"And what can you tell me about Chan?"

"Look Charley, I think I can see where this is going. Can I go try again?"

"Sure. But first, take a seat. I'll let you in on a secret. You can build stronger relations with people in two weeks by becoming interested in them than you can in two years trying to get people interested in you. It's okay to mix in a little self-disclosure, but sparingly at first.

"My most formative lesson in the power of MBWA happened about 20 years ago. I was a fairly new operations manager on the night shift in another plant. I was in a strange place. The hours were unusual and quite frankly, like all managers in a new job, I didn't know what I was doing. We started at 10:00 p.m. and ended at 8:00 a.m. The shift was running so poorly that we would often leave work for the day shift to finish—which was not good.

"One night I was poring over operation reports. We were well below the required performance level in every element: safety, quality and production. Attendance was poor, attitudes seemed worse and the shift supervisors were just lost. I didn't know where to begin. Then I thought about a mentor I had early in my career. I got out of my chair and started walking. That was my defining moment! My feet moved and for the next three hours I walked around the operation talking to people. I took that same walk every day for the next two years. That was when I began to understand the power of communication and the importance of building rapport with people.

"I talked with everyone and soon realized what good people I had. Eventually, they came to the same conclusion about me. They began to give me suggestions on how to improve the operation, and we gave consideration to every one of them. We implemented many of the things they came up with and quite a few are still in place today. The people that do the work know more about their job than we will ever know. We need to harvest that knowledge.

"We communicated results back to them, recognized them for their ideas, and thanked them for their input. I found that when you recognized someone for an idea, there was always a bigger, better idea coming down the road. It starts to snowball. What started for me that night became a lesson in MBWA, and how it built rapport. I came to understand that my management style was participative, that is I not only needed, but I wanted people involved. It also started to make management fun."

"Management fun. Fiddle-de-dee, fun for you," Linda thought, channeling her best Scarlet O'Hara impression.

Linda was beginning to understand. She tried the approach suggested by Charley and found she enjoyed it immensely. She also realized that she and Charley were building some rapport along the way.

Every morning at 7:30, Linda would take a walk and talk to people. Not about work, but other stuff...their families, hunting, fishing, sports, pets, movies, whatever they were interested in. She developed a genuine interest in her people and actually learned a few things along the way. After a couple of weeks she believed she could talk to just about anyone and was feeling more relaxed in the operation. Inevitably work talk also became easier and an extension of the relationship-building. She really was starting to have fun.

True, her first job had been a disaster. She lived management at its worst. She now realized a big part of that failure was her own inability to build any rapport with her people. She saw the error of her ways and vowed never to repeat those mistakes. She was beginning to think that her first job was only a prelude to the lessons she was learning now.

She arrived in work areas about the same time every day and noticed that people had things to tell her. The routine of MBWA had become much more than that to Linda and to the people with whom she was forming good human relations. She noticed something else when she returned from a day off—her people actually missed her.

During her time at Perryman-Willis, Linda never saw her team as being the answer to her problems. She rarely came out of her office and when she did, it was all business. She didn't try to get to know them and didn't allow them to get to know her. "MBWA and rapport building, no way!"

These people at Cobart did their jobs very well. They did not need a lot of motivation, but what they did need was some interaction with the people they reported to. "They want to feel human," she thought. "They also want to know that I am human as well and that what they say is important."

One day Charley was waiting in her office when she arrived after a morning of MBWA. "Well, I see you are building rapport with your people," said Charley with a grin. "I'm getting great feedback from them. They tell me you are approachable, genuine, willing to learn—and nice. Don't underestimate the importance of being nice. They really like you. I think you have learned the first of the four building blocks. Remember communication builds rapport. You need that in place before you can tackle the other three."

"You know, Charley, I also found that people want to get to know me. So a little self-disclosure does go a long way. I own a Jack Russell and Sue in the staging area for standard units has a Jack Russell. We were comparing dog food. Sam is a Jets fan and you know my Dad had season tickets for 10 years and that made me a Jets fan. Joe in prefabrication has a daughter who has applied to UConn..."

Charley looked pleasantly bemused. "Remember to not have an ulterior motive. Your intent is just to get to know your people and let them get to know you."

"What's next?" asked Linda, not trying to hide her excitement.

"Training," said Charley.

"And what does training build?" asked Linda.

"Training builds skills. Are you ready?"

BUILDING BLOCK 2: TRAINING

Training Builds Skills

"Train people well enough so they can leave,
treat them well enough so they don't want to."

Richard Branson

Linda was surprised by the number of hours that were dedicated to training. Besides the required safety, Occupational Safety and Health Administration (OSHA) and equipment handling certifications, she noticed there was a personalized training plan for each employee.

"If we're going to exceed our goals," said Charley, "we need to make sure every employee is trained to handle all the responsibilities of his or her job—as well as the jobs of the person on each side of them.

"You may have noticed how seamless things appear around here. The main reason is training. We cross-train everyone to do at least three jobs. It's a huge competitive advantage. Most managers don't realize their main role is not to make a product or deliver a service. It is to train and develop their people.

"This concept actually came up about five or six years ago and I was not the one who thought it up," Charley continued. "I have to give credit to Denise in special products. She said that she could significantly improve her efficiency if she fully understood the jobs being performed on each side of her. It still works and when someone is absent we have coverage."

"I get that, but how can you afford to train people constantly?" asked Linda. "We average 35 hours a year for every employee. And what if we do all this training and they leave?"

"The more important question is what if we don't train them and they stay," Charley replied. "It depends on how you value training. Many business owners consider training a cost. If you do that, then training gets watered down or cut entirely. It becomes a task that has to be checked off. It's a paper game.

"Training is an investment. It's the best way to build your people's skills. Let me draw this analogy: Every employee has a piece of string. The day-one employee has one-foot of string. They need a lot of supervision. You can expect them to do the basic elements of their job—but nothing more.

"The very experienced worker has 50-feet of string. Besides doing their basic job, they identify small problems and fix them before they become big problems. They implement ideas to improve the operation. They make adjustments on the fly and they act as mentors to the new people.

"I remember you telling me you spent most of your day putting out fires at your old job. If your people continuously bring you all their problems to solve, you're going to lead a miserable existence. Remember I said management can be the best or worst job in the world? It seemed like you had a whole crew of day one people, even though many had been around for years."

Linda nodded, remembering her struggles at her old job.

"Training allows you to take an employee with one-foot of string and start feeding them more string," continued Charley. "When someone gets 50-feet of string they make decisions that are in the best interests of the business—just like a business owner. They are fully engaged and empowered. You've met many of these people on the shop floor. They are confident and they take a tremendous amount of pride in their work. And your job becomes easier and more fun.

"Our job is to take a person with one-foot of string, and continue to build their skills until they have 50-feet or 100-feet. If you think of it in those terms, then training makes sense. Our focus as managers is to train our people so they reach their potential in their job—that they know how to do their job in the safest, most efficient manner. And if your people know that it's your intent to make them great at their jobs, they will buy-in to the training.

"Linda, as a manager, would you rather lead a group of people with 50-feet of string, or people with one-foot?"

"That answer is pretty obvious," said Linda. "I've seen what happens when you lead a group with one-foot."

"It's all about building their skill set—putting more tools in their toolbox, more clubs in their golf bag, more arrows in their quiver. I'm all out of clichés," said Charley. "But come with me, and I'll show you an example of an employee who had 50-feet of string and acted like he only had one-foot. We may need to reel him in a little bit."

The shop foreman, Jack, was waiting in Charley's office. There had been a near incident with one of the special products molding machines that Linda knew was quite large, ran hot and had a lot of moving parts. An unsafe act had been committed by Chan and Darlene. The violation was on a type of horizontal molding machine. The pre-trip was not completed, the equipment temperature was set too high, and the material was fed at a higher rate than specifications—all in the interest of saving time.

"Hell!" said Charley. "I'm surprised that machine didn't explode!"

Chan was a senior employee and Darlene had been around for only four months. Linda knew that if Charley was going to get upset about anything, it was safety.

"Is the incident report complete?" Charley asked.

"Yes, and it shows two people with safety violations," said Jack. "Which include pre-trip, equipment temperature and materials handling. Fortunately no one was injured."

Charley put his face in his hands, let out a deep breath and seemed at a loss. It was the first time Linda had ever seen this reaction, but she noticed Charley recovered his outward composure quickly.

"Okay, bring them in," said Charley.

Chan and Darlene came into the office, heads down and nervous.

"Chan, what happened?" asked Charley.

"I took a shortcut," said Chan. "We were running behind schedule and I decided to take a shortcut so we could gain some time and make our deadline. It was a mistake, no excuses. It's all on me."

"I know it's all on you. That's a given," said Charley. "Where did you get the notion that taking a shortcut was okay? Did your training give you that option?"

"I knew it was wrong when I did it. No excuses. It's all on me," said Chan again.

"Well, not only did you put yourself at risk, but you put Darlene at risk as well," said Charley. "Darlene, as far as safety is concerned, even if the president orders you to take a shortcut, you have the power to refuse. Do you understand?" Darlene nodded her head.

"And as for making your deadline, what's the procedure if you don't think you will make a deadline?"

"To tell my supervisor," said Chan.

"Right," said Charley. "Chan, I'm very disappointed in your decision-making. You're one of my leaders on the floor and if you're making bad decisions, then I'm worried that other people aren't buying into the safety culture we've built here.

"Here's what I need you to do," Charley added. "At the open-book meeting tomorrow, I need you to tell this story to the entire group. Tell them your thought process in compromising safety in order to make your deadline. If you made this decision with your experience and background, then other people might be doing the same. We need to address this issue and put it to bed once and for all."

Charley excused Chan and Darlene and turned to Linda. "All the training in the world doesn't ensure that people won't make bad decisions when faced with job pressures. So, along with skills training there needs to be constant communication about the gray areas that employees face when doing their jobs. But one positive thing happens in the workplace when something significant like this occurs; it gives us the chance to know our people better and in turn they get to know us better."

"So, how do you think Chan likes having to get up in front of the group to do a mea culpa?" asked Linda.

"I'll bet he'd rather discuss a mental mistake than an accident or injury," said Charley. "Besides, if you are going to have honest communication with your people, some of it is going to be uncomfortable."

"Most companies have it backwards," Charley said. "They communicate their expectations, say they did it and call that communication. Then they're surprised when the numbers don't improve. There needs to be ongoing communication and it has to be the `right' communication."

"And what's the `right' communication?" asked Linda.

"Do you balance your checkbook every month?" said Charley.

"Sometimes," answered Linda sheepishly.

"Well, that's what we do here. We open up our checkbook to our people. Once they understand how their business makes their profit, they can figure out the impact they make to the bottom line. They make suggestions on how to improve the numbers. It's called open-book management."

"How does it work?" asked Linda.

"Tomorrow morning I'll show you," said Charley.

Opening the Books

"The more people understand what is really going on in their company, the more eager they are to help solve its problems."

Jack Stack

At 7:00 a.m. every employee is gathered in the large conference room. There are pastries, fruit, granola bars and coffee available on a nearby table.

The data show fires up and Charley shares the October results.

It's a monthly "State of the Business" report. He starts with safety, stating that there were no OSHA reportable injuries for the month. A little extra money would go into the employees' bonus pool. That gets a round of applause.

Then Charley asks Chan to get up and describe the near-accident and his thought process in making his decisions. The room falls silent as Chan goes through the scenario point by point and admits his poor decision making in that instance.

Charley thanks Chan for his candor and ends by stating that there is never a good time to make a bad decision, especially when it comes to safety. He reminds the group that the average cost for an OSHA Recordable injury could wipe out their gain-sharing program this quarter, not to mention the pain and suffering to the injured employee. "Hey, we all know better than to take shortcuts," said Charley. "The time you save cutting corners doesn't come close to the impact of a serious safety accident in people's lives."

He then reviews quality, equipment breakdowns, customer service issues and operating ratio (OR). OR is a key metric used to describe profitability. The people seem very interested and talk about ways to make improvements in the business.

During a short break Charley gives Linda an overview of the "Open-Book" concept. "These meetings are held the second Wednesday of each month, after all the numbers are in and we have something meaningful to share with everyone. Linda, keep in mind that our people run households. They understand income, budgets and saving for the future. All the things businesses do. They know what they pay for electric power. And rent. Why shouldn't they know what we spend? The more they know about our finances, the better decisions they make on the shop floor. We don't want them to check their brains at the door. We want them to bring their brains to work."

"And how do you think the Chan situation went?" asked Linda.

"It depends, but what we did was take an unfortunate situation and turned it into a learning experience. When people are trained and held accountable they change. Even in these circumstances. They also will see that we care about them. When something significant occurs, good or bad, it gives us the chance to know our people better and in turn they also get to know us better."

"Aren't you concerned that people will take some of the information and use it to compromise your efforts?" Linda asked. "I thought some of the numbers were confidential. You shared all kind of statistics, even quality issues and number of defects."

"That's always a possibility. A few people may take advantage of the situation. But remember that 95 percent of the people are going to use the information to give you great results—which will more than offset anyone trying to undermine you. It also shows our people that we trust them with this information and that we value their judgement. People are capable of great things if you give them the right information.

"Open-book management requires a general understanding of revenue, total cost and net profit." Charley continued. "If what we're doing doesn't increase revenue, control cost or increase profit, we ask ourselves why we're doing that activity. And we need to keep it understandable and leave out all the accounting verbiage used in corporate-speak. Through open-book management, people know where they stand and how they contribute. They learn how their work impacts the bottom line."

Charley continued. "It also gets the wheels in their minds spinning. Everyone is now trying to think of ways to make things better. They will share ideas with each other. They are empowered to try things as long as they don't adversely impact safety or service. You have already seen some of their best ideas and they certainly did not come from me."

"So open-book management is the reason for our great results?" asked Linda.

"It's not the only reason but it's a big part of it. I just share results," said Charley. "Some managers think they can just tell people what to do, and how to do it, and head back into their office. I thought early in my career that I knew what was best and after being proven wrong countless times, I realized there was a better way. You tell your people how the business is doing, and then ask them for their ideas. You begin unleashing your people's potential. They figure things out and come up with ideas that had not even occurred to you."

"Charley, that sounds great," said Linda. "But won't people get tired of trying to come up with the next great idea?"

"Well, first of all, these aren't all great ideas. Some are good. Some are bad. Some are crazy. The important thing is that we have our people thinking about our business and ways to improve it. My job is to take those ideas and start building a raging fire of energy that drives our organization forward. It's very powerful and it's the third building block."

"What is it?" asked Linda.

"You know how to start a fire, don't you?" asked Charley.

"Yes," said Linda, a little confused.

"Well let's go fire one up," said Charley. "The meeting is about to re-start."

BUILDING BLOCK 3: RECOGNITION

Recognition Builds Behaviors

"Research indicates that employees have three prime needs:
Interesting work, recognition for doing a good job,
and being let in on things that are going on in the company."

Zig Ziglar

Linda reflected on the past few months and what she had learned. Her job was enjoyable and rewarding. Earlier, Charley mentioned the 2 by 4 approach to building a business. That was the last time she heard that phrase. It included communicating to build rapport and training to build skills. Now he wanted her help in building a fire. Whatever that meant. But she was about to find out.

In college she was taught theory, concepts and measurement. There had been very little on the subject of people. Now, working with Charley, she realized everything was about people. She remembered a bumper sticker she once read: "The world would be a better place without all these people." A lot of business people still thought that way. She was convinced now that they were wrong. People really are the solution.

Linda and Charley's conversation was interrupted by loud clapping and a chant of "Char-ley, Char-ley, Char-ley."

"It looks like I'm being summoned," Charley said with a wide grin on his face. "I can't keep my fans waiting."

Charley entered the conference room with a dance reminiscent of a bad YouTube video. He moved slowly and deliberately, and with each exaggerated move drew a loud cheer from the crowd of employees. Linda had never seen employees having so much fun at work. As the applause subsided, Charley got down to the business at hand—Recognition.

He started with birthdays and years of service and was sincere in his praise for each employee and his or her contributions to the business. Linda noticed Jets tickets going to Samuel, a restaurant card to Rosa and passes to an art exhibit for Melanie. Charley knew his people and their tastes and it was obvious that they appreciated the consideration.

Then he told a story.

"Frank Marcozzi, one of our largest customers, was told that a special order for a construction project would not be delivered until Thursday. Due to time constraints, contractors, and a number of other cost issues, Frank needed his product by 8:00 a.m. the next day, which was Wednesday. Frank called for me, but I was downtown at the monthly contract review.

"Sarah took Frank's call and could tell he was frantic. But instead of asking if she could take a message, she told him I was not in and asked what she could do to help. Frank then explained his predicament for the following ten minutes as Sarah listened and took detailed notes.

"Evidently, one of Frank's people talked to someone in our shipping department and they had not been as helpful as they could have been. And we'll address that situation later. Sarah told Frank she would call him back within 30 minutes. She then called Jack and explained the seriousness of the situation to him. She told Jack she had promised the customer she would get back to him in 30 minutes. In 15 minutes, Jack called Sarah and explained what he had done. Jack had rearranged another job, which had a later deadline and put additional people on Frank's job. He told Sarah the job would be completed by the end of the day and Frank would get the material delivered on time. Sarah then called Frank back, apologized for the inconvenience, and told him his materials would be delivered the next day by 8:00 a.m.

"When I found out later, I called Frank and asked if everything worked out. Frank wanted to know where I found people like Sarah and Jack. He was even a little apologetic. He said he might have been a bit abrupt when he spoke to Sarah. The order arrived in perfect condition and on time. Sarah and Jack and his team had saved him a substantial amount of money and aggravation. I would like to point out a few behaviors that made this situation a win-win.

"First, Sarah took ownership of the situation. She could have taken a message and waited to see me later that day. If she did, we would have missed that deadline.

"Second, she got people involved early in the process. If there's a problem, the more people we get involved, the better. Because Jack was involved early in the process, he and his team were able to make adjustments and meet the deadline.

"And third, she stayed in communication with the customer. It's important that the customer is kept updated during the process. We may be putting a great plan in place to deliver his product on time. But if the customer is not aware of it, they will still have worry and anxiety, even though they will get the materials on time.

"Folks, Frank Marcozzi gives us over three million in business a year and Sarah, Jack and his team just impressed the hell out of him with their rapid response to his problem. You turned a potential disaster into a service grand-slam."

Charley then invited Sarah, Jack and his team to the front of the room. Charley handed out gift cards and led a round of applause for the group. "For your outstanding achievement in the area of customer service. I am so proud of you," he said.

When the meeting was over Charley and Linda walked back to Charley's office. "That was awesome," said Linda. "I've never seen people worked into a frenzy like that."

"We've been doing this for a long time," said Charley. "Years in fact.

Recognition creates the energy that drives an organization forward. You tell your people what behavior you want. And when they give it to you, you have to make a big deal about it. Many organizations miss that step. They expect good behavior, but when they get it—nothing happens. Do you know how demotivating that can be for people? It's like your team wins the Super Bowl and everyone walks off the field like it's just another day.

"I equate it to building a fire," said Charley. "A fire is very hard to start. It takes a lot of effort at first to get the tiniest spark. You have to tend that spark to get the smallest flame. Once you get the flame, you feed it with small twigs and dry grass until the fire starts to grow. As it grows you pile on bigger pieces of wood until you have a raging fire. Once you have a raging fire you can throw a huge, wet log on top and it will burn.

"It's the same with recognition. You have to do a lot of work up front. You recognize small efforts and small accomplishments. As the fire begins to grow, you recognize larger efforts and larger accomplishments. Once that fire is raging you get what you saw today: groups of people coming together to solve a customer's problem. We now have a raging fire when it comes to recognition. But 10 years ago, we would have recognized Sarah for just taking a message. As I said before, recognition builds behavior."

"At my old job, people told me that their paycheck was the only recognition they needed," said Linda. "How do you manage people like that?"

"Well, they may say that, but I think every person has a flame inside them that craves recognition for a job well done. We don't start that flame but we can certainly build on it. It's called pride or ego and I haven't met many people who don't have it. If a person has an ounce of pride, I can work with them.

"Of all the approaches management takes to motivate people, appealing to their pride is the most powerful. Some use fear, intimidation, or position, but appealing to a person's pride is the only way to get consistently great results. Look who we recognized today. They were prideful people. Do you think we could have gotten those same results if we used fear, intimidation or rank to manage them? No. The best you can get with fear, intimidation and rank are mediocre results. And short term at that. And what fun is that?

"Most people trudge into work every day, punch in, punch out, go home, drink a few beers and watch the ball game. Not our people. Yeah, they probably drink a few beers and watch the ball game, but they don't trudge. Why? Because that flame inside challenges them to do great things at work.

"By the way, how was your date last night?" Linda had mentioned it in passing the night before and was surprised he even remembered.

"Great, we went to the new seafood restaurant and Dave was quite interesting. We are going to the game this weekend, so that's a second date..."

"Linda, one more thing that management needs to recognize. They need to recognize that their people have interests, responsibilities and a life outside of work. Please let me know if work ever interferes with that balance. What I mean is that when someone has the appropriate amount of off work activities, they are better employees. It is one thing that many places of business frequently fail to understand.

"My first management position was in a large company and it was there that I learned some very valuable lessons about what not to do. Some companies get it, but oftentimes management in a large organization creates a work environment where people feel they don't matter. That has been the downfall of more businesses than people will ever know. It is not lack of profitability that wipes out an organization, but it's the lack of caring about people that dooms a company. To care about people means caring about more than just work."

"Never heard it put that way before," said Linda. "Usually all that matters is work. Do your job and go home."

"Work and outside of work are directly related," replied Charley.

"You know, Charley, it does go along with everything else around here. I think a lot of companies would like to create that atmosphere. They just don't know how."

Later that day, Linda thought about that concept. Companies say people are their most important asset and that they want their people to have work-life balance. But then they ignore the fact that someone has worked five consecutive 12-hour days. Charley not only said it, but he modeled it as well. He walked the talk. It did not mean that people did not occasionally work 12-hour days, but management needed to recognize those efforts and show their appreciation for it.

To Charley, work-life balance was more than a phrase. It was part of his management philosophy. Something that had actual meaning. If it was possible, Linda felt even more recognized and appreciated after this brief conversation. Not only as an employee, not only as a human being. But both.

Charley believed in real estate enterpeneur Gary Keller's statement, "Work is a rubber ball. If you drop it, it will bounce back. The other four balls—family, health, friends, integrity—are made of glass. If you drop one of these, it will be irrevocably scuffed, nicked, perhaps even shattered."

BUILDING BLOCK 4: ACCOUNTABILITY

Accountability Builds Synergy

"Accountability breeds response-ability."

Stephen Covey

Early January and the weather was cold and dreary. The mood inside the plant was even worse. Linda was to meet Charley in his office at 7:00 a.m. and she knew the meeting was with Dan, a two-year employee in standard units.

Dan had forced this level of accountability and had write-ups, formal warnings and two suspensions in his file for safety violations, attendance, failure to follow methods and overall performance. All of this despite the fact that he demonstrated competency in his job and understood what he was being held accountable for. There had been no change in Dan's behavior.

Present at the meeting were Dan, his union steward, Denise, Charley and Linda. Charley gave a thorough review of Dan's work history. He took his time, emphasizing key reoccurring behaviors. There was little emotion. The key message was that this was Dan's job and his responsibility.

"Dan, we have provided you with everything you need to be a productive employee. As I review your file, it appears everything is in order and you have demonstrated the ability to apply the training and perform your job safely. Is there anything I've missed or we need to know?" Charley asked.

Dan admitted that he did not need any more training and that his attendance and work performance could be improved upon. "No, and I really do not have anything else to add," Dan said in a manner that was part sarcasm and a little rebellious.

Charley suspended Dan for five days without pay. Dan could file a grievance. But even the union steward knew that with all the documentation Charley presented, such action would not result in a different outcome during a next-level appeal process. Linda knew that Charley did not enjoy these types of confrontations. "Linda, like I've often said, there are two responsibilities of every employee: come to work every day and do the job to the best of his or her abilities. Most people get pretty close; Dan is a long way off and does not seem to care about changing his work habits."

Linda had a conversation with the union steward afterwards and she was quite candid. "Charley does not want to use the hammer. It is a very selective device. But if he has to, I have never seen him hit the wrong nail."

Denise said this with a little shake of the head. Linda thought this a compliment, but also confirmation that this place of business was very even-handed—even generous. But this was still a place of business and she thought that companies must never lower their high standards because they owe it to their employees to be sustainable. People count on businesses to stay in business.

Dan did not return to work. He called in mid-week and said he had notified the union and had decided to quit. While Charley had been forced to terminate a fair number of people in his career, he claimed he never fired anyone. "They fire themselves," he said.

"What about Dan?" Linda asked later that day. "Is there something we missed?"

"Excellent question," answered Charley. "Whenever an employee is fired or quits, we have a responsibility to find out why. We need to ask ourselves if we gave that person every opportunity to be successful. Have you noticed the mirror on the back wall? Go over and take a look." Linda walked over and looked into the mirror. "What do you see?"

"Well, me of course."

"Linda, if you are ever considering getting rid of someone, take a look at yourself in a mirror and ask if you have done everything in your power to make them successful. If the answer is 'yes,' then you will be able to live with your decision and let a person go.

"I think in Dan's situation, we did. We communicated with him and he understood the expectations around here. We trained and retrained him. We also recognized him when he did a good job. He knew what was expected of him and chose not to do it. Who knows what was going on in his head? It's tough to predict human behavior. But I don't think he had pride in his job. For whatever reason, Dan was not ready to commit to his job. His behavior proved it. When you have someone like that in your organization, you have to let them go. They are draining the organization of its energy. It's Synergy.

"Synergy is created when the whole is greater than the sum of its parts. In other words, when two or more people combine their efforts, they can accomplish more together than if you added their accomplishments achieved separately."

Linda had heard the term used since college. Something like one, plus one, plus one, equals four. The whole is greater than the sum of its parts. But she had never really thought about it at Cobart. She now realized that had been happening each day at work. There were times when orders were processed with unsurpassed quality and production that did not seem possible.

"As a manager, you need to protect and grow your business' synergy," said Charley. "It's the force that gets you great results. I talked about building a raging fire through recognition. Well, someone like Dan is a wet blanket that can douse that fire. You have to be vigilant about people who can destroy your synergy and hold them accountable. Your people are looking at you to protect the synergy they have worked so hard to create."

And it was not as if Cobart was always one big happy family. The employees at Cobart argued occasionally, held grudges and at times did not like one another; Linda smiled a little and thought maybe they were like a real family. But one thing always happened. The work got done. The job seemed to rise above petty differences and the personalities that sometimes clashed.

Linda realized that synergy cannot occur without a high level of accountability. "We can never lower our standards or expectations for high levels of performance," said Charley. "If you want the whole to be greater than the sums, then each part of the system must be a highly functional unit."

Charley took a non-authoritarian approach to leading people. "I don't need to tell everyone I'm the boss," he said. "They know that. The first time I pull rank on someone I lose some respect—respect that took a long time to build. I need to respect people as much as they respect me. What I try to do is serve my people. I give people the tools and authority to do their jobs and then turn them loose."

"I do not think I've heard serve and manage used in that manner," said Linda.

"Well, to manage is to serve," answered Charley. "If you serve the people who work for you, you can get great results."

Linda had a little bit of a headache as she walked to her car. It was like her brain was expanding. It probably was. Every day Charley made her think differently about business. She had never thought about people in the manner Charley did. "Our job is to get people to perform work at a level that even they did not think possible," he said. "It's about giving them the tools to be successful and then letting them go."

Accountability Needs Boundaries

"To me there's no creativity without boundaries. If you're gonna write a sonnet, it's 14 lines, so it's solving the problem within the container."

Lorne Michaels

The next day, Linda was conducting the pre-work meeting as

Charley looked on. It was a review of the previous day's results.

"Has this morning meeting thing always been in place?" asked Linda.

"Not always," said Charley with a laugh. "There's a story behind this meeting."

"You seem to have a story behind everything," said Linda.

"We talked yesterday about not pulling rank, but serving your people and getting great results."

"I remember," said Linda.

"Well, during my first week here I noticed something odd happening at the 7:30 start time. Nothing. Nothing was happening. There were a couple of people in the break room or outside, some just chatting about whatever and a few in the restrooms. At 7:45, people began shuffling to their work area.

"My first instinct was to do what most managers would do—go berserk—and start yelling and screaming. But I was a little more experienced by then and I knew I had just discovered an opportunity to improve my business.

"At that time we had 36 hourly employees. So I grabbed a calculator and multiplied 36 times 15 minutes per day and got 9 hours. I multiplied that 9 hours by 250 work days in a year and I took our average hourly rate, which at that time was $28.50, and that came to $64,125. I had just discovered a $64,000 business opportunity.

"The next day I called a meeting for 7:30, and told my people to be there on time. I told them I had an idea that could save the organization more than $64,000 over the next 12 months. I also told them that some of the savings would flow back to them in the form of a gainsharing program.

"I proceeded to map out the cost of 36 people starting work 15 minutes late over the course of a year. You could hear a pin drop in the room, as the people realized what I was really saying—that they were 'stealing' time and it had to end. The kicker was that even though they were at fault, they were even going to gain from it!"

"Why would you start a gainsharing program after they were all late? That doesn't make any sense to me!" Linda was incredulous.

"I know, crazy, huh?" said Charley.

"Well, I outlined the program parameters during the next two weeks and everyone understood that we would have a communication meeting at 7:30 a.m. each day and that in addition to safety, quality and production, attendance would be criteria in the bonus pool. That morning meeting, which lasted about five minutes, set the tone for the rest of the work day. It helped people to understand their responsibilities."

"Charley, I get that, but how do you know it worked?" Linda asked.

"If I was just measuring profitability I could draw a definite correlation, but that was not my objective."

"Isn't that what is most important, the bottom line?" Linda asked.

"Ultimately, yes, but that cannot drive every action and intention. We try to share as much as we can and people want to have some degree of control over their work life. We clearly recognize in our personal lives that before any relationship is formed, there is sharing. You saw how a few people were prodded along today by people I refer to as informal leaders?"

To Linda, this was all starting to make a lot of sense. It was like a coiled light bulb that kept circling until entirely lit. "I saw the gainsharing statistics and it looked like everyone received about $375 last quarter. Is it worth it?" Linda asked.

"Well if you do the math, it makes good business sense, but there is more. Accountability needs boundaries and since everyone is engaged in the process our safety and quality numbers are the best they have ever been. The savings there has been tremendous, all because of our people. We never need to concern ourselves about getting off to a good productive start to the day either.

"I will confess something to you," said Charley. "I always need to have some control over workplace events." This struck Linda as a little out of place. Charley had appeared to have little regard for lines of authority and her expression said so. "If I cannot exert influence, in my way, I would be lost. You've seen some of the tours with higher ups we have had around here, correct?"

"Yes, but I never thought they were served up with the fanfare I expected," replied Linda.

"There's a reason for that, and it's not that I want to appear contentious. I just want them to see what happens here every day.

"I have not told you, but I have been offered a promotion to the corporate office."

Not knowing what else to say, Linda faked a smile and said, "Charley, that's great, congratulations!" Charley's expression looked strange.

"I turned it down," and not waiting for a response, went on. "I fit here. I can make a difference and what we do here may look like just parts, fabrication and molding, but it is much more to me. The promotion was to a job in contract review. There are plenty of people who can do that work and right now, it just did not fit what I want and need to accomplish. I think most of all I need people. I like people and the daily interaction that goes with it. What we need most is management who understands and can pass it on.

"Linda, the four cornerstones?"

"Communication, Training, Recognition and Accountability."

"Do you see how they fit together?"

"Yes, one cannot be done without the others and there seems to be a natural order. Charley, how well do you think other companies do at this process?"

"Well, they have to first recognize how important their people are, therefore, many companies never get out of the starting blocks."

"Guess you like the business of construction parts fabrication?"

Charley liked Linda's inquisitive nature.

"Every business produces something in regard to a product or service. I think that our skills as managers translate into most industries. And it's all about people. I also think you need to believe in what your business does."

Today was one of the busiest of the year and there were two deadlines that had to be met. In her old job, her boss and everyone else would be breathing down her neck, calling every 30 minutes with most likely a mid-day conference call to discuss progress. Not here. Charley let his people work and be accountable for the job at hand. The confidence he had in them was astounding. He listened, valued people's opinions and never interrupted them. He felt what they had to say was important.

The drive home, which Linda defined as decompression time, was much different from just a few months ago. She thought about the work environment and how it was unlike anything she had experienced. She noticed earlier in the day the ease with which Charley walked the production floor. It seemed he had not a care in the world, but Linda knew this not to be the case.

Accountability Reveals Defining Moments

"When a defining moment comes along, you can do one of two things. Define the moment, or let the moment define you."

Tin Cup

The next day, Linda was doing some MBWA as the shift began and noticed something out of place on a machine used to mold special products. Larry and Joan were the operators and had completed their pre-work inspection. It was small, almost unnoticeable, but a securing bolt at the top of the machine appeared to be damaged.

"We should get the plant engineering person down here," Linda said to both machine operators. The piece could probably hold until evening, but if repaired, production would be delayed for a line of six employees in various stages. She knew an end of day deadline did not overrule safety. Larry, the PE guy, inspected the damage, said it could be a problem and it would take an hour to fix.

"Please take care of that immediately," Linda said without hesitation.

There was some discussion about how to prevent this in the future, but the focus was on adjustments for the rest of the day. There was no finger-pointing—only let's get the job done. When the shift continued one hour later, Linda worked with everyone to finish the job. She felt accountable to fix the problem and complete the work order.

While most of these jobs were union positions, there was emergency contractual language to meet customer commitments. Linda was not doing a lot of work, but everyone would have said she helped them to work smarter. Charley never came out of his office. He did not have to. He was too busy congratulating himself on his amazing judge of character.

At the end of the shift the job had been completed and was ready for shipping. Linda was covered in dirt and grease, but she actually felt good after a hard day of intense thought and labor. A nice business suit ruined. Well, maybe not that nice. Linda remembered talking about the job to one of her friends and they started to discuss business attire. "They don't sell a lot of industrial type clothing at Nordstrom's," she replied laughingly.

"You know what just happened?"

"I'm still trying to figure that out to tell you the truth," Linda replied, as she walked by Charley upstairs.

"Never underestimate the power of coincidence and the importance of recognizing when it happens," said Charley. "I think if you keep an open mind, you will discover a coincidence almost every day. What you do with it, is up to you. A coincidence oftentimes results in a defining moment. And with that comes an overwhelming sense of accountability."

"Thanks, does the power of coincidence always end up dirt and grease covered?" They both laughed hard.

On the way home Linda almost cried. Okay, she cried a little.

In the past four months, she had learned more about people than four years of undergrad at a large university, plus three years at her old job. At the same time she was beginning to learn how to tie together book learning and actual experience.

Linda had another enjoyable date with Dave. She also could not wait to get to work tomorrow. This felt a little weird, but in a good way. A year ago at this time she had to force herself into a distant, dreadful memory. It was also a coincidence meeting Charley in the grocery store and she was thankful that her life had gone from so bad to so good. She thought about how her work life during the previous year had impinged on the rest of the hours of the day to the point where she was consumed. The tears she shed that day were of relief, hope and anticipation of great things to come.

The next day Linda realized things had changed. It's like every business owner or manager who walks into their shop or operation can tell immediately how things are going. At this moment, Linda realized how Charley felt walking into work each morning.

"What you did yesterday helped foster the feeling of mutual respect, which is a key component of accountability," Charley said.

"Thanks, and I think I've realized that respect is much more than the position you hold."

"So true," said Charley. "If people know and like you then respect is easier to develop. I have always needed to respect people as much as they respect me; maybe more. Just be mindful that contrary to what you might have heard, it's important that people know and like you. It's not a competitive advantage to be a hated boss. I remember a manager said at an old job that people don't need to like you; they only need to respect you. Well, I do not respect people who I do not like.

"Forget about business relations," said Charley. "This is all about people-relations. Consider this: If you meet a person you don't like, would you go out of your way to be friends with them. Of course not! There's no difference between building personal relations and business relations. It's all the same."

Charley had said quite a few things that really jolted Linda's world. The four cornerstones and the basic belief that people come to work every day and try to do the best job possible. The other was that people needed to be honest. If they made a mistake admit it and move on.

"As long as people worked hard, were honest and committed to do the right thing, they didn't need to worry about making mistakes, or getting fired. People have enough to worry about. Plus, as long as people make mistakes, there will always be the need for management," said Charley with a laugh.

"Go figure," Linda mumbled to herself.

PRIDE

"It is not the broken heart that kills, but broken pride."

Gilbert Parker

"What about trust?" Linda asked several weeks later, during a review meeting with Charley.

"What about it?" Linda was getting used to a little cat and mouse play, as she referred to his antics. Charley always liked, in fact preferred, that people figured things out for themselves. How he never ran out of patience, she never could understand.

"You never mention the word 'trust'. It's all you ever read in books about the best business practices. It's obvious that the people around here have a lot of trust." Charley just listened. "There is a tone around this place that indicates that there is a high trust level, but..."

Charley knew it was time for him to explain.

"Trust is a 'come to work' item."

"What do you mean by that?" asked Linda.

"Most people in business can be trusted. It is well known that in the general context of the word, most business leaders understand its importance, but it is still a come to work item."

"Then how come so few people seem to bring trust to work with them? In my last job, I never knew what was coming next, or so it seemed. What do you mean a come to work item? I thought trust was hard, that you had to earn it and it was easy to lose?"

"Don't get me wrong here, trust is very important. But when you started your old job did you automatically trust everyone?"

"Well I guess not, I didn't really think about it," replied Linda.

"Right, you didn't even think about it, until it became an issue." Charley could sense a little confusion from Linda.

"You mean I can't just wave a magic wand and my people will trust me?" said Linda.

"What managers need to do is act in a manner that is honest and reasonable. In time, people will come to trust what you say and this will be reinforced by your actions. People trust at different levels. If we're so busy trying to build trust it will be like being a coach and focusing too much on winning and not on the fundamentals that result in continuous improvement.

"So it's a come to work item in terms of my personal behavior. Trust is defined with words like honesty and reputation and phrases like doing what you promise. Those are all givens to me. If I have to think about being honest, then I am in the wrong place. I choose to let trust take care of itself.

"Linda, you know the four cornerstones?"

"Of course, Communication, Training, Recognition and Accountability."

"They are just a process," said Charley. "See, many companies just deploy programs and procedures and expect that they will work. And they do work for a while to some degree. But leaders oftentimes wonder why they need to deploy program after program, year after year. It needs a glue to hold it all together."

"But what could be more important than trust?" asked Linda. "And what is the glue?"

"Remember the fire we built?" asked Charley, referring to the building block of recognition.

"Of course," said Linda.

"How about the result when a company places profit first and people a far second? Someone once said we run into problems because someone's dignity has been kicked around. While the four cornerstones are a process, they affect people and when this happens you stir emotions."

"You have the reputation as a fixer of sorts," said Linda. "It sounds like everywhere you have been in your career, this has worked. How can it be so easy?"

"Easy?" replied Charley. "Far from it. This is one of the most sophisticated management styles ever developed. The four cornerstones look easy. Through the complications and demands of business they can crumble quite easily. You know what I do? I stay at it, because I know it works. I am persistent.

"Once the four cornerstones are in place and honestly deployed, our people provide the glue that makes the structure strong. Management just needs to continue to be supportive and enthusiastic."

"And what do you call the glue?" asked Linda.

"Linda, you know the big sign we have when you enter the building?"

"Yes, it says: "We Build People Here.""

"Well, that's it in a nutshell. That's what we do here. We build people. We build people through communication, training, recognition and accountability. They are the cornerstones, but there are two glues that hold it all together. One comes from your people and one comes from you."

"I'm all ears," said Linda. "What comes from my people?"

"Pride," said Charley.

"Pride?" repeated Linda, as an inquisitive look crossed her face.

"Yes, pride," said Charley. "Pride is one of the strongest forces in nature. It has driven people since they lived in caves. It's that inner voice that challenges us to do better, reach higher and strive to improve.

"Pride caused our founding fathers to declare their independence from England. Pride propelled our soldiers to storm the beaches at Normandy. And pride landed a man on the moon. Pride is a flame burning inside each of us. A manager's job is to fan that pride. Like I've said before, if a person has an ounce of pride, I can work with them. So you see, a manager's job is to build people. Build the people and you don't have to worry about the business succeeding.

"When I saw you in the grocery store that day and offered you a job, I saw that your only problem was that your pride was damaged. You were smart and motivated, but your pride was hurt. That's a problem for many people. Their pride has been trampled on, ignored, or attacked. And I wanted to show you through Communication, Training, Recognition and Accountability that you could rekindle that pride in yourself—and in your people.

"It's all about helping your people reach their potential. I used to coach a lot of youth sports when my kids were young. I learned early on that the key to success was making every player better every day. Forget about wins and losses. Focus on making your team better every day and the wins will take care of themselves. Legendary basketball coach John Wooden used to say that if his team played to their potential, it didn't matter how well his opponent played. So focus on making your people better.

"I used to tell my little leaguers that if I scheduled them against high schoolers they would never win a game. And if I played them against five-year-olds, they would never lose one. So all you can focus on is making yourself better. That's all you have control over. And every day your people either get better or worse. No one stays the same.

"The problem is that businesses want results yesterday. They don't recognize continuous improvement—even though continuous improvement is the main component of any quality movement. But most businesses only care about daily results. And if you don't hit your numbers, you're a bum. Hard work is nice, but it doesn't cut the mustard. You either made the goal or you didn't.

"When I first came to this plant, all the numbers were in the tank. We weren't doing anything well. The first thing I did was retrain every worker on the floor. My boss called me in after about a month and told me he was disappointed that I hadn't turned things around yet. I told him that the numbers were going to get worse before they got better. He was stunned and upset. I told him we were retraining everyone and that took time and money. He didn't want to hear that. I told him once the training took hold, we would begin to improve and we would get results that the organization had never seen before. That was a bold statement, but that's exactly what happened.

"Results take time but you're seldom given the time to implement your plans by upper-management. That's the dilemma that every front-line manager faces. But you have to stick to your guns and believe that developing your people will be successful in the end.

"If you focus on making your people the best they can be in the areas of safety, performance, quality and customer service, what employee will argue with you? Focus on making your people `great' and see the support you get from them.

"Focus on their pride and empower them. When you expect your people to do great things—they do great things. You get what you expect and more.

"People also want to know what's going on. They want to know what they do impacts the bottom line. They want to know that their ideas are implemented, or at least considered. They want their boss to recognize when they do a good job and point out their mistakes. They want to be proud of the work they do.

"Imagine this place if everyone worked to their full potential. Even though we do excellent work here, we are only operating at about 90 percent efficiency. That next 10 percent is what I'm focusing on. The answer is out there on the shop floor. My job is to find it."

Linda realized how little she knew about management when she arrived at Cobart. She had always thought that successful management was as easy as getting a degree, landing a job, being the boss, and watching the results roll in. Now she knew better.

"Linda, what motivated you to come to work today and do the job to the best of your abilities? Because you trusted me or you had pride in your job? Like I said trust should be a given. Pride is something you hold within. Which is more powerful?"

"So I think I understand the glue now," said Linda.

"Not so fast. There is still one more lesson I want to share with you."

"More glue?" Linda smiled.

"More glue," said Charley, smiling back.

CARING

*"People don't care how much you know until
they know how much you care."*

Theodore Roosevelt

"Linda, besides Sarah and myself, who was the first person you met around here?"

"The foreman, Jack, and the two of you were talking about some operations problem. If I remember correctly you asked about his son. I did not understand then, but I do now. I always admired the strong relationship you and Jack had."

"When I first got here, Jack would not even talk to me before his start time. His work was good, but he was abrasive and unfriendly. I had been here about two months when Jack's mom, Lucy, got sick. She had been admitted to an intensive care unit at a hospital in Phoenix. We were two days from inspection on an enormous project and Jack's input during this process was crucial.

"The building was fifteen stories, in the middle of the city, and we were in meltdown pre-inspection mode. Our prefabricated construction units were a major part of this phase of the inspection and despite all of the conformance testing, it was still a relatively new process. On that day, Jack told me about his mom. He was almost in tears and up to that point I had never seen any semblance of emotion out of him. He said he could work the next two days, but after the inspection, he would need to travel to Phoenix.

"I told Jack to leave immediately. We would survive and when he had a chance, to just send me an update. Things were never the same between us after that."

"What changed?" Linda asked.

"I didn't really think about it at the time, but people noticed that

Jack left at a crucial time for our operation. Since Jack was an influential leader, word spread that I had told him to go take care of his mother when he was also needed here. The message was that I cared about my people even at the expense of the business. Not the other way around. A genuine caring attitude is your choice. When it comes from us, with no expectations, people change.

"But do you want to know something else about management that many people never seem to grasp? People notice what management does. If you have 30 people in a group and something happens, they will look to see how you react."

"Somehow, it does not seem fair," said Linda.

"It's not. Who said being a management person was fair? But it can be very rewarding and there are always opportunities. During difficult times especially, people want to see if you really care about them. Remember when we talked about defining moments. Well that was another, and luckily I made the right decision.

"Jack's mom is fine now, by the way. But the bottom line is let people know you care about them and they will care about you, as well. Oh, and that little thing called an inspection...passed with flying colors."

"So it's the four cornerstones of Communication, Training, Recognition and Accountability. And the glue that holds it all together—Pride and Caring," Linda said thoughtfully.

"I call it my 2 by 4 approach. A very powerful building concept. It works for building houses and for building people."

That night Linda's head was spinning. She knew her time with Charley would soon come to an end. She also knew she was prepared for whatever her future held.

WHERE IT STARTED

"I have good news and bad news. The good news is that the secret to people relations is really easy to understand and not really a secret. The bad news is that if it was easy, anyone could do it."

Charley

It was now early March and Linda had seen five months of the 2 by 4 approach in action. It was modeled every day. There was little talk about money or profits or corporate pressures. Linda knew by the corporate guests who Charley entertained that he was getting his fair share of recognition. Whenever this happened, Charley would brush it off. Linda was amazed at how his focus was on his people and not his own ladder-climbing. The concentration was on his 2 by 4 approach.

Charley at times seemed more a facilitator than a plant manager and as always his job looked easy. As he told her many times, "Management can be the best job in the world or the worst. The difference is how well you build your people."

Linda now knew the secret. Charley's form of management was quite sophisticated. He always put in the time and effort to understand what was going on in the operation and how people reacted to different situations. It was the opposite of the old 2x4 which encouraged managers to whack their employees over the head with a 2x4 when they wanted things done.

Later that day, Linda had a question for Charley. "That night in the grocery store, after only a few minutes, you planned to offer me this job. I'm really appreciative and I have a completely different outlook on my role as a manager. I know you were my dad's best friend, but it wasn't as if you even knew me. Both of you always appeared to be concocting something when you were around the house."

"You thought your father was some kind of insurance guy, right?" said Charley.

"Yes, he was a manager in some claims clearinghouse or something like that."

"Linda, your father was the greatest leader I've ever met and that is a story in itself. I was a new supervisor in that call center. The corporate office wanted to close it because it was performing so poorly. That meant 220 people would be out on the street. The place was unprofitable and a dismal place to work.

"Your dad inherited a real mess. I think he was brought in to be a temporary stopgap before they closed the facility and relocated him to some other location. You never moved did you?"

"No, of course not," said Linda. "I never knew much about my father's work. He always came home happy and he rarely discussed work."

"He promoted me to lead supervisor. Guess who taught me everything I know? Your dad! That call center became a success story and a gem of the company. People still talk about it. It was my introduction to the 2 by 4 approach. It was amazing how your father turned that place around. After just a few months you could walk in and feel the difference.

"After that I got an opportunity to become a manager and your dad urged me to take the position. He told me, once you understood the 2 by 4 approach, you could make it anywhere. As you know, we stayed close and oftentimes discussed these concepts. Your dad was my mentor. And luckily I've had the chance to be yours. When we met in the grocery store, I had a feeling your dad had brought us together. You learned the 2 by 4 approach a lot faster than I did. I think you've learned who you are now and will be successful anyplace you go."

Linda was speechless. She got up, put her arms around Charley and cried tears of happiness.

THE NOT SO SECRET BOX

"There's a time in your life where you're not quite sure where you are. You think everything's perfect, but it's not perfect. Then one day you wake up and you can't quite picture yourself in the situation you're in. But the secret is, if you can picture yourself doing anything in life, you can do it."

Tom DeLonge

A few days later Charley and Linda began their weekly review. This time Charley sat behind a medium-sized plastic box. He had a grin on his face.

"Am I supposed to guess what is in the box?" Linda asked.

"You already know. It's what we talked about for the past five months. So it's not really a secret."

Then Charley started to pull things out of the box:

A pair of old work boots; a little worn in the soles. Or, as Charley called them ... rapport builders. "Use these to build relationships with your people. Manage by walking around. Communication builds rapport."

A ball of string. Charley rolled it around like a baseball. "Every management person has a ball of string." Linda was smiling, but she knew to let Charley finish this one as he was on a bit of a roll; pardon the expression. "Your job is to get rid of as much string as possible. I am going to jump to a likely conclusion. If at the end of the day you have less string on your ball, then you have probably done some good things for your people and your business. Training builds skills."

A safety recognition letter. "Recognize the people who are making your job easier. Build a blazing fire through recognition. Recognition builds behaviors."

A performance appraisal. "Make sure you measure what people are being held accountable for. Accountability is not a bad word. People want to know where they stand. Once they do, they will take pride in their job and you will get results you never imagined. Accountability builds synergy."

And don't forget the glue that holds it all together: Pride and Caring:

Pride: A weekly operations summary. "It's the result of the four cornerstones when they have been implemented effectively and honestly."

Caring: Charley pulled out a `thank you' card which Linda had given to him a few weeks prior. Inside it read: "Charley, I cannot thank you enough for this opportunity. I have learned so much about people and how vital they are to a business. More importantly, I have learned about myself and have gained the confidence and the skills to be successful wherever I go."

"I showed this to my wife," Charley said. "She was touched and so am I."

Charley then withdrew a small box. "This is for you." Linda opened the box and inside was a leather billfold with a mirror and an inscription on one side. "If you ever wonder what is wrong with your people—look here first." "Your father gave that to me years ago when I moved on. It has been an inspiration to me and I would like to pass it on to you."

The next day at 9:00 a.m. they sat in Charley's office. Linda noticed that Charley was a little nervous. It was performance review time. Linda reviewed the elements herself and gave a rundown on strengths and areas needing improvement. When she finished she expected some comment, but Charley had something else on his mind.

"Linda, I think your performance evaluation speaks for itself. There is a job opening at the plant over in Woodbury. It is twice this size and they need an Assistant Plant Manager. The Plant Manager is Don Allen. Good person, but a little bit of a hard ass. I have reviewed your qualifications with the corporate office and they are prepared to offer you the job. I certainly think you can make a big difference there. The pay is considerably more than what you make now. The job starts on March 24 and it is a permanent position. It's a good facility and they make tensile strength products like rebar and reinforced steel. Questions?"

Linda would wait until tomorrow for follow-up questions. She knew Charley would not recommend her for a position unless she was qualified.

"I know I am supposed to say let me think about it, but my answer is I'm in, and I appreciate the opportunity. Thank you, Charley... for everything."

The following day Charley came into Linda's office. "Let's take a walk."

As they entered the operation, all the employees started clapping. Many hugged Linda and wished her success in her new assignment. Linda just looked at Charley.

Then Chan stepped forward and handed Linda a parting gift—a piece of a 2 by 4 signed by all the people on the floor. It included a plaque that read:

Linda, thanks for all your help and support.
Good luck in your new assignment and remember:

"We Build People Here."

www.ingramcontent.com/pod-product-compliance
Lightning Source LLC
Chambersburg PA
CBHW021039180526
45163CB00005B/2193